4 BRANCHES to SETTING and ACHIEVING GOALS

4 BRANCHES to SETTING and ACHIEVING GOALS

Dennis Petillo

MARILEE Publishing
Altadena, CA

MARILEE Publishing

4 Branches of Setting and Achieving Goals
Copyright © 2021 by Dennis Petillo

All rights reserved. No part of this publication may be reproduced, distributed, or transmitted in any form or by any means, including photocopying, recording, or other electronic or mechanical methods, without the prior written permission of the publisher, except in quotations for critical review by reviewers, as permitted by copyright law. For permissions, contact the publisher, "Attention: Permissions Desk," at the address below.

Marilee Publishing
PO Box 238, Altadena, CA 91003-0238
www.marileepublishing.com

ISBN-13: 978-1-953569-90-5 (Paperback)

Library of Congress Control Number: 2021935951

Book Cover Design: David Kitchen
Production: Marilee Publishing

Printed in the U.S.A.
First Printing, 2021

Ordering Information: Special discounts are available for volume purchases by schools, corporations, associations, and others. To place an order, call (562) 548-2284 or contact publisher at the address above.

This book reflects the authors' present recollections of observations and personal experiences over time. Some names and characteristics have been changed to protect the innocent or guilty, and some dialogue and events have been compressed. Both the publisher and author(s) regret any unintentional harm resulting from the book.

First Edition

DEDICATION

To my mother, Dominica Petillo,

my dad, Robert Petillo and

my sons and daughters.

TABLE OF CONTENTS

Introduction	ix
Chapter One: ASK	1
Chapter Two: PERSISTENCE	9
Chapter Three: PATIENCE	13
Chapter Four: SERVICE	17
Reflection: A P P S.	21
Testimonials	25
Amado Nervo: The Secret Within	31
Acknowledgments	33
About the Author	35

*"We have a source that is very generous.
Come to him for all your needs."*

– Anonymous

INTRODUCTION

This is a short chronicle of my journey to learning the importance of setting and achieving goals. Think of a tree branch's job, which is to provide a way for tree leaves to act as a net for sunlight.

Trees use the sun to help create a process called photosynthesis. Without the photosynthesis process a tree cannot grow or ultimately survive. I was not aware of the many benefits of setting goals, until I became a member of the Rosicrucian Order.

In goal setting, there are many areas in my life where I have evolved. I was like a tree, which my branches needed to capture what I describe as the "sunlight of the spirit." Being a member of the Toastmasters also helped me become aware of the importance of goal setting.

I was born in Dangriga Town, which is located in the southern part of Belize City. One of my goals was to migrate to the United States. With the help of my mother I was able to accomplish my goal. Five years after I arrived, while watching sports on television, a commercial aired which stated, "join the Navy and see the world." It was then that I decided to join Navy. I have been observing immediate family members, friends, and many others not knowing how to set and achieve goals. They were like trees whose branches were not catching sunlight. I decided to write this book to help others to understand my thoughts of how I learned to set and achieve goals. This may help them and others become more productive citizens.

Like the many tree branches on a tree, human beings have many different thought processes and belief systems. This book will explore four elements that are important in setting and achieving goals. The acronym APPS describes these elements best. The elements are; ASK, PERSISTENCE; PATIENCE and SERVICE. Our goals will always originate from our thoughts. The thoughts we focus on will always come into existence.

Most material things we have possession is proof this is true. For example, the clothes we are wearing at this present moment, we consciously or unconsciously first had to think about wearing them, before making the decision to actually wear them.

Let's explore how my life journey impacted my understanding of how APPS serves as the branch that supports us in helping to set and achieve our goals.

CHAPTER ONE

ASK

The largest branch to setting and achieving goals lies in the power of thoughts and asking! According to the National Science Foundation, a person thinks between 12,000 to 60,000 thoughts per day. Our Devine Being always listens and grants us our request. If we do not ask, we will not receive. Certainly, we have all hard the phrase, "Ask and you shall receive." No matter who we are, how old or young we are, setting and achieving our goals begin with asking. We must, however, display positive thoughts and a positive attitude.

While employed by the postal service, I had set goals, either verbally or mentally. My goal was to learn much as I could in the US Postal system. I was able to work in several work sites compared to some of my co-workers who labored 30+ years in only one unit. I worked in an area called the Mailing Primary. This was where we sorted mail by hand. Nowadays, most of these employees have been replaced by automation. Machines require less man power and processes more mail per hour. I was a safety captain and liked working in this position. It gave me an opportunity to visit other units to present safety talks. It also gave me a chance to leave my unit for two hours on certain days.

I worked in a unit called the PAU Dock. PAU stood for Permit Acceptance Unit. This is where the customer brought mail either in postal bags, trays or on wooden pallets. Along with this mailing, the customer brought a form to let us know how many pieces of mail they were shipping. It was our responsibility to verify if the amount was correct. If there were less pieces indicated on the statement, we deducted from the total cost. If there were more, the customer had a choice of taking back the pieces or paying the additional cost.

I also had the opportunity to work in an area that was called the Registry, where all valuable mail was processed. This was mail that included gold coins, watches, ring, bars, etc. This is where I met a man named Mr. Pennywell. Everyone in my unit liked this gentlemen because he was positive. One of his favorite mantra was "It is another beautiful day." He said these words upon entering the worksite through our eight hour work day. Some of us had consciously or unconsciously processed this phrase while at work. Some of us responded to Mr. Pennywell by repeating his exact words.

There were few days my co-workers and I were not motivated to work hard. We didn't socialize like we usually did and production was a little low. We often had these experiences after a three-day holiday. It could have been because we ate or drank too much or were too well rested. I recall after Mr. Pennywell would arrive on the job site and said, "It is another beautiful day," we became more motivated. We socialized more and production increased. The reason why this happened is because positive thoughts led us to positive experiences. So, a message to all of us . . . think positive. Why? Because, there are many benefits. We simply have to ask and think positive thoughts. We will be healthier, happier and will be able to achieve our objectives. If we do not ask, we will not receive. No matter who we are, or how old or young, we can set and accomplish our goals!

There are a few quotes which state this. Abraham Lincoln stated, "That people have achieved success and goals are proof that others can." Famous Comedian George Burns' goal was to become an actor or a comedian. He was triumphant in fulfilling his objectives. One day while on an episode of the Johnny Carson show, Johnny asked Burns why he became a comedian. Burns replied, "I couldn't make money lying in bed." He also told Johnny, one day while at the bar, the bartender told him that his glass was empty and if he needed another one. Burns jokingly replied, "why would I want another empty glass, pour some of that good stuff in my glass."

Exercise: Get a pen and paper and write down all of your goals.

If we do not ask we will not receive. No matter who we are, how old or young, we can set and accomplish our goals.

Simply ask, either verbally or mentally. Why? Because our divine self always listens and is ready to grant us our request. Especially when it comes to goals that are reachable. There is a universal belief, which states, "ask and we shall receive."

Part of this method involves using our imagination.

Albert Einstein, referred to as a genius who invented the theory of relativity said, "The true sign of intelligence is not of knowledge, but of one's imagination."

French Military Leader, Napoleon Bonaparte, said, "Imagination rules the world." Every thought we focus on for a period of time reproduces itself in a physical form!

Asking for what we want relates to the power of

thoughts. As mentioned earlier, the National Science Foundation found that an average person thinks between 12,000 to 60,000 thoughts per day.

Every thought has a tendency to reproduce itself in a physical form. Some thoughts are too weak, or maybe too complicated to ever reach the physical stage. However, but a clear thought, repeated again and again, is almost certain to create a replica of itself sooner or later. There may be a long interval of time, but a clearer non-competitive thought will always manifest physically.

Let me share a true story that will make this clear. There was a young man who was out of work and needed a job badly. He heard of the power of thought and tried to employ it to create a position for himself in the business world. He had no idea of what kind of opportunity would present itself. Not wanting to block out any possibilities, he began to confine his visualization to a picture of himself sitting in a private office; his office. In his mind, the office had four walls, a window and a small desk. As days and weeks went by, he continued his visualization faithfully, every day. He kept adding to the picture.

Gradually, larger pictures appeared on the wall, the desk became one made of carved wood instead of the simple metal, which he had first conceived. As the office grew larger, his own ideas about it expanded. He thought, "why not have a closet where I could keep an extra suit in case I should have to stay in town for the evening?" Having gone that far, he thought of a dressing room and bath in a little annex to the office. He visualized bookshelves on the wall behind him and a large picture window to the right. Thus, his visualization changed and expanded. He kept faithfully at his daily meditation and never despaired as the weeks went by. Eventually more details started to creep into the picture; more than he had intended. For example, although he was in New York and expected to work there, he could see a palm tree swaying outside the window.

It was about this time he landed a job, a good job, with a simple office, with just four walls and a metal desk. It was nothing like the picture in his thoughts, but it was a job. So, he was satisfied and gave up his visualization.

Fourteen years later, however, having become quite successful, he bought a home in Florida. It had a large living room with picture windows. One day as he sat there at his a wooden carved desk, which had come with the house, he idly gazed out of the window to his right. It had suddenly struck him. It was a palm tree swaying outside the window. This was a replica of the room he had visualized many years before. True, he had thought of it then as an office, not a living room. What about the book cases? Well, they there behind him, next to a dressing room and a bath room beside it. And, of course, next to it, a window with the image a palm tree swinging in the breeze outside. He realized, he had unconsciously attained all that he thought of years ago.

We must try to avoid chaotic thinking and try to think logically. People who think chaotically are like those who wave their hands in the dark, unaware of the objects they may hit. Since we cannot avoid thinking, we should at least learn to think in a positive manner. We are living thoughts. It is extremely difficult to control the incessant stream of our thoughts. This is the substance of our consciousness, which flows from our mind into space. If we could control all of them, we would indeed be superwomen and supermen. But let us do what we can. As soon as we are aware of negative thoughts, replace them with positive thoughts. Replace aimless thoughts with precise ones. Each person, being different than any other person, should devise his or her own special pathway of positive and logical thinking.

Avoid untruthful or distorted thinking. How many secrets of bad luck can be explained by distracted thinking: observe as far as we are able, the consequences of untruthful or distorted thoughts are sometimes called prejudice. Erase jeopardizing our own future. Stop releasing dark dangerous thoughts for these come back like a boomerang in the form of bad luck. Of course, it is not easy to think positive. Most people are so crippled by their unconscious thoughts and prejudices. They are not aware they don't know if whether they are thinking truthfully or not, Therefore, when things go wrong, they are not aware of the connection to the belief that "if we ask we shall receive."

> "Ask and it will be given to you
> Ask and you shall receive
> Seek and you will find
> Knock and the door will open to you."
>
> Matthew 7:7

CHAPTER TWO

PERSISTENCE

We must be persistent, persistent as tree branches; more so, as persistent as tree roots. Do things on a daily basis that will help set and achieve goals. We must do the work. No matter what obstacles we experience in life, we must seek out our goals and keep our eye on the prize. Roots of a tree have to seek out water and certain minerals. Before leaves can harvest carbon and energy, the tree trunk must be started. The adaptability of a tree is amazing. Whatever conditions exist, roots are persistent in find any climate for growth; even in a tiny crack of rock on a mountain side or pavement on a highway.

Let's take a look at the present moment in our life and ask ourselves; am I persistent in reaching my goals now. Whether it is paying a bill, attending school, or planning for a trip, we must do the things that help us achieve our goal. Some of us have obstacles in our lives keeping us from accomplishing our intent. No matter what, let us continue to be persistent.

A baby learning to walk is a good example of how to be persistent. While learning how to walk, the baby attempts several times to get up and walk. He or she will fall but gets up and tries again. Even after several attempts, along with the encouragement from others, the baby begins to walk. Let's continue to be persistent.

Suggestion: Use a vision board to help stay focused and persistent in achieving goals. The board can be the size of a sheet of paper or can be larger or smaller. Write a phrase or post a picture of whatever goal we want to achieve. Next, and very important, place your vison board some where it can be easily seen on a regular basis. This reminds ourselves of the goals. The board can be in our bedroom, office or in a school folder. The more we focus on whatever we want, the more it will come into existence. Reflect on all the achievements you have accomplished in the past. It is because you were focused and persistent.

There is a yearly event that young girls and boys take part called Career Day. This event takes place in different parts of the world, including the country of Belize. This is where the child wears uniforms depicting the profession they want to achieve as adults. Surveys have shown children who took part in career days, now working adults, seem to be more successful in reaching their career objectives. The reason; they were focused and persistent.

Adapting a positive attitude helps us stay persistent. A benediction sent into the world is the purest and finest form of thought energy. Our own projects can grow by benediction. Unfortunately, people become so beset by personal problems, which seldom occurs to them. The desire for advancement, better social position or the approval of others dominate their thinking. This causes confusion. Ignoring these tendencies is impossible. Trying to rid oneself of it is futile.

The best course of action is to steer away it. It is a matter of taking better direction. No one becomes perfect overnight. This does not mean we will no longer make mistakes. Through time, however, we will become aware of the laws of energy and begin to handle our thoughts with grated competence. We will find our whole life changing for the better. We will become happier, better adjusted and more at peace with ourselves and others. Our personal power and environments will begin to grow. This happens when we sincerely and faithfully adopt positive attitudes.

Let's imagine ourselves achieving our goal is. By

doing this, we will be able to imagine the end results. For example, if the objective is to become a teacher, imagine yourself in the classroom, studying to become a teacher. Imagine graduating, wearing a cap and gown. Imagine the diploma in hand with a smile on your face. Imagine being happy having accomplished a major goal. Finally, imagine being in front of a classroom teaching students.

Write and create a bucket list. The purpose of a bucket list is to remind ourselves of our goals. Write down your goals and look at the list on a daily basis. Demi Lovato, singer, song writer, actress and television personality, at the age of 17, tweeted, "One day I'm going to sing the national anthem at the Superbowl." In 2020, At the age of 27, she sang the National Anthem at the 54th Annual Superbowl. Persistence was a key.

When writing and setting our goals, we must be specific. If the intention is to become a teacher, define what type of teacher. Will it be a Math, English, Social Studies, Science, History or Music Teacher? If the goal is to become a Doctor, stipulate if it will be a Pediatrician, Cardiologist, Chiropractor or Dietician. Then, set that goal and stay focused and persistent in achieving it.

We must be persistent as a tree. A tree will simply not quit. It persists. It doesn't see obstacles, only opportunities. Sometimes, people will simply give up when life is hard. Quitting must never be an option.

CHAPTER THREE

PATIENCE

We must continue to be patient. Trees do not grow overnight. Growth requires patience, lots of it. Even growing a Bonsai tree is a practice in patience. Many people get frustrated when growing a bonsai, or any tree for that matter, because they want to see results right away. But, like the slow growth of trees and their branches, we don't always see our goals manifest right away. It takes patience and time.

"All achievements require time," said American Writer David Schwartz. We must continue to show patience. It takes patience to graduate from High School or College. It takes patience to learn how to drive a car. When meeting our significant other, some of us had to wait months or years to hold their hand, or to even go out on a first date.

Think of a fruit tree. Take a seed of a fruit, dig a hole in the ground, place the seed in the hole, cover with dirt and water it. With the help of Mother Nature, it will take months or even years for that tree to grow and bear fruit. We have to have patient.

In March of 2020, I helped my friend Eddie. His mom, Mrs. Harris, told me her freezer was not freezing food. I drove to her house to diagnose the freezer. After running several tests, the diagnosis was that the compressor needed to be replaced. I informed Mrs. Harris, and with her approval, we decided to replace the part. After purchasing the compressor, my helper and I observed that one of the connections on the compressor and the freezer were different. One was of copper and the other was of aluminum. After trying on several occasions to solder these two connections, I was able to solder the two pipes, but there was a leak.

After a week, Eddie became frustrated and told me to forget about fixing the freezer. They had become impatient. Instead, his mom decided to buy a new freezer. I had purchased the compressor and did not want my money to go to waste. I texted Eddie a couple of times to let him know I will pick up the freezer and compressor. He told me when the new freezer arrives, he would call for me to pick them up.

Three months later, Eddie texted me that the new freezer had less shelves. He said they had changed their minds and decided to fix the old freezer instead. My helper, a gentleman and myself went to get the freezer from Mrs Harris. It gave me more time to work on the appliance and monitor the progress.

On my first attempt at installing the compressor, I saw there was a leak. I waited a couple of days and asked for guidance and assistance from the Divine to help me stop the leak. I tried again. After my second attempt to repair it, I was able to stop the leak. Patience had paid off. I learned that asking, persistence and patience can occurs at the same time. Then, there comes the part about not giving up.

While charging the freezer with Freon, a bee landed on the manifold of my charging instrument. Being afraid it would sting me, I took the cloth and swapped it off the manifold. The bee fell on the ground. I gently stepped on it, thinking that the bee's life on this earth was over. It laid there, but to my surprise the bee starting moving. Soon, it got up and started moving in circles. It then started walking away and then disappeared out of sight. That bee, struggling to stay alive, reminded me that in life we will encounter obstacles and challenges. However, we must not give up.

If we ask for help, be persistent and patient, we can achieve our goal. The key is to ask for guidance and demonstrate faith and hope.

"All great achievements require time."

- Maya Angelou.

CHAPTER FOUR

SERVICE

The fourth branch to setting and achieve goals is being of service. We give trees water so they may grow. Trees grow and give off oxygen that we need to breathe. Trees also provide food, protection and homes for many birds and mammals. In essence, tree are being service to the living world as we know it.

Being of service means giving back to our families and communities. We should do this before, during and after setting and achieving our goals. Being of service is doing something for a person, a group, a community, a cause or a belief. It means we've chosen to engage in "giving back" without the expectation of receiving.

Service is the activity done for the benefit of others, which actually results in self benefit. American Poet Maya Angelou said "what we learn we are to teach;

what we get we are to give." This is a good thought to ponder when we are setting our goals. Helping others is important when setting and achieving our goals. As we set our goals, think of the people we have helped along the way. Think of the people who we have done a favor for, who one day will return that favor to help us achieve our goal. This is why we should understand the benefit and universal action of "giving and receiving."

There is action in giving and receiving. Take for example a baseball player. We should not go through life wearing baseball gloves on both hands, only prepared to receive the ball. Baseball players wear a glove on one hand and none on the other. The player throws the ball with one hand and catches the ball with a glove on the other hand. In other words, the player gives and then receives.

The universe loves a cheerful giver. As the bible puts it in Corinthians 9:6-7 "... each one must give as he has decided in his heart, not reluctantly or under compulsion, for God loves a cheerful giver."

Being kind and giving opens up a world of opportunity. Being of service sets the foundation for setting and achieving goals. In order to receive though, we have to give. The more we deposit, so to speak, the more we receive. Think about this concept as it relates to our trips to the bank. What we continue to deposit into our bank account will be there for us, if and when we need it. Subsequently, a time will come when we will need to make a withdrawal from our bank account.

If we are of service to others, others will be of service to us. We will be treated as we treat others. If we smile people will smile back at us. If we are kind, people will be kind to us. If insult or harm anyone, likely, we will be harmed and insulted. If we love, we will be loved. This is based on universal law that states "give and you shall receive."

Let's ask ourselves, are trees being of service? Well, let's think about that. Life may not exist without trees. Trees produce most of the oxygen that humans and wildlife breathe. Trees absorb carbon dioxide from the atmosphere and then release oxygen through the process of photosynthesis. Furthermore, trees provide a supply of lumber, seeds, and fruit. Trees break the force of wind and rain on soil. The decay of their falling leaves from their branches are absorbed by the earth and enrich the soil. More so, dead trees fall, get buried in the soil and eventually provide fossil fuels like coal and petroleum.
    It goes without further illustrating, trees are definitely being of service. We too can benefit from being of service.

"Ask what thou wilt"

by Amado Nervo, Mexican Poet

If at this moment thou should present himself before thee, a being clad in white respondent with magnificent light and he was to say to thee, ask what thou wilt it shall be granted to thee. Thou wouldst hasten without doubt to ask the best things. Will then that miraculous being exist within thyself and has the power to give thee whatsoever thou ask of him. Only beforehand thou shouldst now full well what it is that thou desires truly knowledge that seems easy yet which very few humans attain and after that thou knowest though shouldst ask the God within with such assurance ask if the miraculous man all dressed in white who would lour thy faith by the prestige of his external presence. Think that thou art unfortunate because though ignores that which thou canst do. All is thine and thou art dying of longing. The stars belong to thee and thou hast no light on thy heart. All nature wants to give itself to thee as its lord and master and thou weapest at disdain of a woman. Ask what thou wilt for all shall be granted to thee.

REFLECTION

ASK, PERSISTENCE, PATIENCE, SERVICE

There are physical laws or cosmic laws that govern the universe and humankind. These laws are the driving forces of APPS; Asking, Persistence, Patience and Service. The divine laws were designed and created by God, the Divine, the Architect omniety or by any other name we wish to call our higher power. If we are truthful in our intention to achieving our goals, we should be open to study these laws. With the knowledge, understanding and respect of these laws, we can live in harmony with each other, and with life and all events. This doesn't mean there will be no challenges. Yet, if we become familiar with these universal laws, the challenges can be invigorating, rather than defeating. The great law of thought governs the spiritual universe. It is the answer to setting and achieving our goals. These laws function through our universal mind, which flows in and through us. It is a creative and intelligent power. Whenever we use our mind, we are setting into motion the creative power and energy of the universal mind.

The universe is one complete, creative and dynamic whole. All of our thoughts seek to manifest and become creative once placed into the universal mind. Every thought we think struggles to become a reality and is destined to manifest. Our thinking brings about certain realities and experiences.

The powerful law governing thought was written early upon the pages of wisdom in the book of life. When the conscious mind produces a thought, it is delivered to the unconscious mind affected by it. Our thoughts become critical to our ability to setting and achieving our goals.

There are people who are beginning to think independently, activate and employ the laws of thought. The proper use of thought is a learning process. We have to ask for help. It takes time, patience and direction. No person, regardless of how sincere or devoted, is free from failure or faults. Do not berate yourself over this. What really counts is forward progress and commitment to improve.

During a flight to my hometown to Dangriga on a Cessna airplane the pilot humorously asked for a volunteer to be his co-pilot. A young lady and I volunteered. She was chosen. After that experience,

REFLECTION

I kept mentally saying to myself that one day I would love to have a chance to sit in the co-pilot seat. Years later, I received a telephone call from my good friend James. He asked if I could go and repair a refrigerator at Compton Airport. My answer was yes and gave him a day and time I would be there. While travelling to the airport, James called me. He told me he was not going to be there but that George would be waiting for me at the Compton airport gate.

When I arrive at the parking lot, George was there to greet me. We introduced ourselves and he drove to the building where the refrigerator was located. I observed several Cessna planes on the runway. While diagnosing the problem, I told George that one of my goals was to fly as a co-pilot in an airplane. After diagnosing the refrigerator problem, (another failed compressor), George asked me if I wanted to take a flight in his airplane. My answer? I quickly said yes!

George took me to his airplane. He rechecked to ensure everything was working properly. After I got in and put my seatbelt on, he gave me a headset. I heard every word the person from the tower was saying. We taxied and took off. We flew to San Pedro and returned to the Compton airport. It was one of the most beautiful experiences I ever had. My prior thoughts were manifested and I had accomplished my goal of being a co-pilot.

We can accomplish any goals that are reachable. Throughout time and countless books, we find reference to a Divine Plan and Divine Architect. The term Divine Architect of the universe implies that there is a divine creator or builder. The Divine Architect is who directs the result our goals when we ask for help and are persistent, patient and continue to be of service.

Three different approaches can be taken in bringing about a realization and manifestation of the plan. The first approach is by continuing on the path to an understanding of who we truly are. The second is becoming aware of and identifying with the attributes and qualities of our true selves. A great deal of inner light will begin shining through us. We begin to understand realization of who we truly are. . It's important to give attention to this part of our being every day. Contemplate its meaning. Visualize the possibilities. Ask for what we desire, be persistent in attaining it, be patient for it to manifest and give to others by being of service. And like the roots, trunk and branches of a tree, we grow our purpose by setting and achieving our goals.

TESTIMONIALS:

Mr. Petillo;

Thank you for making the time to speak to our youth business (YBA) student members on the importance of visualizing, planning and exceeding their goals. I felt that your records on PPS 4 to 5 especially timely. Many of our students need constant reminders to be persistent, have patience and to be of service which are truly necessary to become a great person and a strong leader.

Your contribution is invaluable and assists in the continued success of the YBA program. We are truly appreciative of your willingness to give of your time and to lend to enrich the lives of young people. Once again thank you for your contribution.

With appreciation,
Paulo Menchuca
YBA Instructor and Toastmaster

Mr. Petillo.

I wanted to thank you for taking time out of your busy schedule to peak with my "Finance Management and Assessment" class yesterday.

Everyone, including myself, enjoyed your conversation regarding how to meet your goals with the students. You have given them the inspiration to work hard, reach out and know not to be afraid to make mistakes in life but to take baby steps, one step at a time, to achieving your goals.

Your conversation on the importance of public speaking, appreciating the people around you and your own personal experiences as a youth was most inspiring to the students. It allowed them to think about setting goals and taking action in making them a reality.

Thank you so much for your words of wisdom, time, patience, guidance, and support. I hope you enjoyed your time with my students as much as we did with you.

Best,
Jane Nakamo-Nakamoto
Business Teacher/ Academy Business
Downtown Magnet HS

Mr. Petillo,

    I hope you are doing great today. My name is Nancy and I was one of the students that you spoke to yesterday at Downtown Magnet HS. For Ms. Nakamoto's class. I wanted to begin by thanking you for taking your time to speak to our class yesterday. Being a motivational speaker is hard and can be nerve racking. I can understand since I am taking classes for public speaking at the California State University of Northridge as a part of the Police Cadet Academy that I am in. You have inspired many of us, but you have especially inspired me.

    The way you showed confidence, your vocabulary, calmness and body movement grabs the attention of the audience. You reminded us of the first thing we do when we wake up, we think about what will do throughout our day. That's something we all do but don't really pay attention to. We are grateful for the time and effort you took to show your thoughts and experience with greater Los Angeles chapter. Since we are entering a new phase in our lives, your comments were very useful and I believe we can benefit from your speech. Your enthusiasm is contagious and we hope to use your suggestion in the future.

    I also want to personally thank you for your service to our country. Please accept our sincere appreciation for the presentation you made to our class about your life story and experiences.

Best Regards,
Nancy Solano
Downtown Magnet HS

"A Teacher was once a Student, a Winner was once a Loser, an Expert was once a Beginner. But all of them crossed the bridge called LEARNING.

— Anonymous

AMADO NERVO
"THE SECRET IS WITHIN YOU"

Seek within thyself the solution of all the problems, even those which they think is most material and external. Within thyself is the secret always; within thyself are the secret. Even in order to open for thyself a path through the virgin forest, even to build a wall, even to stretch a bridge, thou must first seek within thyself the secret. Within thyself already are all the bridges stretched out.

Within thyself are cut already the underbrush and the cloying vines that close the way. All the architectural structures are already standing within thyself.

Ask the hidden architect; he will give thee all his specifications.

Before going to see the sharpest ax, the strongest pick the most serviceable spade; enter within thyself and ask. And thou shalt know the essential part of all the formulas will be shown to thee and thou shalt be given the strongest of all tools. And though shalt succeed constantly since within thyself and ask. And thou shalt know the essential part of all the formulas will be shown to thee and thou shalt be given the strongest of all tools. And tough shalt succeed constantly since within thyself thou bear the mysterious light of all the secrets.

ACKNOWLEDGMENTS

I am spiritually blessed to be encouraged and supported by family, work colleagues and friends.

Thank you LaSandra Downs, Sherrie Norwood and Beverly Williams for your wonderful assistance helping me to put my words into writing; David Kitchen, for helping me to bring this book to life; to all my Toastmasters for showing me the way and to all of the school teachers and personnel for your testimonials and for inviting me to speak to your students.

ABOUT THE AUTHOR

Dennis Petillo was born in Dangriga Town, located in the southern part of Belize. His first three years of schooling was at Sacred Heart. He transferred to Primary Holy Ghost, where he graduated. In grade school, one of his goals was to play the part of a wise man in the Christmas play. He believes this was the start of his wanting to be a public speaker. Although his wish came true, he found that he only had one line. He was so happy to have been selected that told his mom and sibling's the good news. When they came to his play, they saw him proudly, but nervously make his theatrical debut, and delivered his one line . . . "Mirth," he said. After the play, his brother Vivian joked that he had invited the family to a play where he said one word. Little did his brother and mom know was that was the beginning of his speaking career.

At 16, with the help from his mother, Dennis migrated to Los Angeles, joined the Army National Guard and served ten months. One day, while watching sports on television, a commercial aired and he saw the words "Join the Navy and see the world!" Two months later, Dennis joined the Navy, was stationed on the USS Okinawa and was assigned to the engineering division. His tours included Hawaii, Guam, Korea, Hong Kong, Japan and the Philippines. After four years he was honorably discharged in May, 1980. Six months after his service, Dennis accepted a job with a refrigeration company and then attended Los Angeles Trade Technical College, graduating with an A.S. degree in Refrigeration and Air Condition. Later, he would be employed by the U.S. Postal Service, Dennis is currently a member of Toastmasters International, where he served as Area and Division Director and became a Distinguished Toastmaster, the highest award recognition. As a member of National Speakers Association, Dennis is a "Goal Inspirer," helping others achieve their goals. Dennis is now a motivational speaker and helping others set and achieve their goals using his concept of APPS.

MARILEE Publishing

www.ingramcontent.com/pod-product-compliance
Lightning Source LLC
Chambersburg PA
CBHW070040070426
42449CB00012BA/3119